Summer Fun

BARBOUR
PUBLISHING

ISBN 978-1-60260-019-5

Published by Barbour Publishing, Inc., P.O. Box 719, Uhrichsville, Ohio 44683, www.barbourbooks.com

Our mission is to publish and distribute inspirational products offering exceptional value and biblical encouragement to the masses.

Member of the
Evangelical Christian
Publishers Association

Printed in the United States of America.

What's the best thing about summer? All the *fun* you can have!

This collection of Bible games and boredom-busting activities is sure to add a ton of enjoyment to your summer months. Whether you're in the car on a long trip to your family vacation spot or you're stuck inside during a thunderstorm, there's something here for everyone.

Short instructions accompany most puzzles and activities. Check your completed puzzles with the answers in the back. Share jokes, trivia, tongue twisters, and riddles with your family and friends—and be sure to fill in the blanks of the silly stories with the craziest words you know. Read them out loud for even more laughs!

Sharpen your pencil—and let the fun begin!

FINISH *the* VERSE

USE THE CODE CHART BELOW TO FINISH THE
VERSE ON THE NEXT PAGE. (EXAMPLE: K=24)

	1	2	3	4	5	6	7
1	A	B	C	D	E	F	G
2	H	I	J	K	L	M	N
3	O	P	Q	R	S	T	U
4	V	W	X	Y	Z		

JOKE BREAK:

Why did the cow enroll in drama class?
To become a moo-vie star

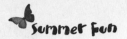

"I AM NOT _____ _____ _____ _____ _____ _____ _____
          11   35   21   11   26   15   14

OF   THE   _____ _____ _____ _____ _____ _____,
               17   31   35   32   15   25

BECAUSE   IT   IS   THE
_____ _____ _____ _____ _____   OF   _____ _____ _____   FOR
 32   31   42   15   34   17   31   14

THE   _____ _____ _____ _____ _____ _____ _____ _____ _____
             35   11   25   41   11   36   22   31   27

OF   _____ _____ _____ _____ _____ _____ _____ _____   WHO
       15   41   15   34   44   31   27   15

BELIEVES: FIRST FOR THE _____ _____ _____,
                         23   15   42

THEN FOR THE _____ _____ _____ _____ _____ _____ _____."
             17   15   27   36   22   25   15

ROMANS 1:16

5

CROSSWORD

ACROSS

1. "YOU SEE, AT JUST THE _____ TIME."
2. "WHEN WE WERE STILL _____."
3. "_____ DIED FOR THE UNGODLY."
4. "VERY RARELY WILL ANYONE DIE FOR A _____ MAN."

DOWN

1. "_____ FOR A GOOD MAN SOMEONE MIGHT POSSIBLY DARE TO DIE."
2. "BUT GOD _____ HIS OWN LOVE FOR US IN THIS."
3. "WHILE WE WERE STILL _____."
4. "CHRIST DIED FOR ____."

TRIVIA TIME:

An angel started an earthquake by rolling back the stone that sealed Jesus' tomb.
(Matthew 28:1–4)

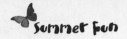

FILL *in the* BLANKS

USING THE WORDS BELOW, COMPLETE THE VERSES ON THE NEXT PAGE.

HOPE   PATIENTLY
SAVED   HE
SEEN   WHAT
NO   HAVE

TWIST YOUR TONGUE:

Kick six sticks quick.

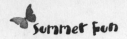

"FOR IN THIS _____ WE WERE

_____. BUT HOPE THAT IS

_____ IS ____ HOPE AT ALL.

WHO HOPES FOR WHAT ____

ALREADY HAS? BUT IF WE HOPE FOR

_____ WE DO NOT YET

_____, WE WAIT FOR IT

_____."

ROMANS 8:24–25

SCRAMBLED VERSES

UNSCRAMBLE THE WORDS BELOW AND COMPLETE THE VERSE ON THE NEXT PAGE.

"SI ETH WLA, ORHTEREFE, SPOOEDP OT HET SMRPIESO FO DGO? TOBALLYEUS OTN! RFO FI A WAL AHD NBEE EGNVI ATHT UCODL RPIMAT FELI, NHET NEGRTSEUHISOS LODUW AECTNYLIR AHVE CEOM YB ETH AWL."

JOKE BREAK:

Knock knock.
Who's there?
Pasture.
Pasture who?
Pasture bedtime. Go to sleep.

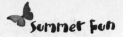

"_____ _____ _____,

_____, _____

_____ _____ _____ _____

_____ _____? _____

_____! _____ _____ _____ _____

_____ _____ _____

_____ _____ _____

_____, _____ _____ _____

_____ _____ _____

_____ _____ _____ _____ "
.

GALATIANS 3:21

WORD LIST

(adjective) _____

(number) _____

(adjective) _____

(adjective) _____

(adjective) _____

(adjective) _____

(noun) _____

(number) _____

(verb) _____

(verb) _____

(number) _____

(verb) _____

(adjective) _____

RIDDLER:

What belongs to you,
but other people use it more often?
Your name.

12

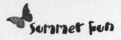 Summer Fun

A LETTER FROM CAMP

Dear Mom and Dad,

I'm having a _____ time at camp!
(ADJECTIVE)

My _____ roommates are a lot of fun!
(NUMBER)

At night, we tell _____ stories and
(ADJECTIVE)

_____ jokes before going to sleep.
(ADJECTIVE)

The food is _____. For breakfast,
(ADJECTIVE)

we had _____ eggs and
(ADJECTIVE)

_____. I ate _____
(NOUN)   (NUMBER)

servings!

During free time, I like to _____.
(VERB)

I am also learning how to _____!
(VERB)

I miss you, but I'll be home in _____
(NUMBER)

days. I promise I'll _____
(VERB)

again soon.

Love,

Your _____ child
(ADJECTIVE)

13

SCRAMBLED CIRCLES

ON THE NEXT PAGE, UNSCRAMBLE THE WORDS IN THE LIST BELOW. THEN USE THE CIRCLED LETTERS TO COMPLETE THE VERSE.

1. EMCA

2. SMEOS

3. VINGE

4. YTR

5. RTCSIH

6. KECSN

7. OYU

8. UJSES

TRIVIA TIME:

Jesus and Peter once paid taxes with a coin found in a fish's mouth.
(Matthew 17:24–27)

1. ◯ _ _ _
2. _ ◯ _ _ _
3. _ _ _ _ ◯
4. ◯ _ _
5. _ _ _ ◯ _ _
6. ◯ _ _ _ _
7. _ _ ◯
8. _ ◯ _ _ _

"SO THEN, JUST AS YOU RECEIVED
CHRIST   JESUS   AS   LORD,
__ __ __ __ __ __ __ __ TO LIVE
IN HIM."

COLOSSIANS 2:6

15

WORD LIST

FIND THE WORDS LISTED BELOW IN THE WORD SEARCH ON THE NEXT PAGE.

LOVE

PEACE

FRUIT

SPIRIT

PATIENCE

HAPPY

KINDNESS

JOY

GOODNESS

FAITHFUL

GENTLE

JOKE BREAK:

What do you get when you put
a cow on a trampoline?
A gigantic milkshake.

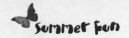
```
M L Y E C D A M J O Y M
N O F L P R P B C K S D
B V M J E J A A Q I E S
G E H S A P T R U N U B
O D A R C V I B R D W S
O M I N E S E T I N S T
D E T M J V N M U E H N
N U R N O O C T B S G Q
E G E N T L E H U S U U
S E U A G N B N M E L F
S R D M M E I W E Y B R
F A I T H F U L C A X U
R N E L P P I C M S I I
H A P P Y V B N D X U T
Y M N Y I S P I R I T R
```

I WILL PRAISE HIM

"AT THIS, JOB GOT UP AND TORE HIS ROBE AND SHAVED HIS HEAD. THEN HE FELL TO THE GROUND IN WORSHIP AND SAID: 'NAKED I CAME FROM MY MOTHER'S WOMB, AND NAKED I WILL DEPART. THE LORD GAVE AND THE LORD HAS TAKEN AWAY; MAY THE NAME OF THE LORD BE PRAISED.'"

JOB 1:20–21

AS YOU GO THROUGH THE MAZE ON THE NEXT PAGE, COLLECT THE LETTERS AND UNSCRAMBLE THEM BELOW.

— — — — — — —

TRIVIA TIME:

Job's wife thought he had bad breath.
(Job 19:17)

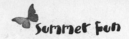

PRAISE THE LORD

ABRAHAM or ABRAM?

ABRAHAM BEGAN HIS LIFE WITH THE NAME OF *ABRAM*. AT SOME TIME IN THE FUTURE, GOD CHANGED HIS NAME. AS YOU GO THROUGH THIS STORY, YOU WILL FIND OUT WHEN AND WHY THE LORD CHANGED THE NAME OF THIS WELL-KNOWN MAN.

"TERAH TOOK HIS SON ABRAM, HIS GRANDSON LOT SON OF HARAN, AND HIS DAUGHTER-IN-LAW SARAI, THE WIFE OF HIS SON ABRAM, AND TOGETHER THEY SET OUT FROM UR OF THE CHALDEANS TO GO TO CANAAN. BUT WHEN THEY CAME TO HARAN, THEY SETTLED THERE."

GENESIS 11:31

 ## TWIST YOUR TONGUE:

Bridget burned bananas and bandannas.
Bandannas and bananas Bridget burned.

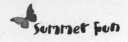
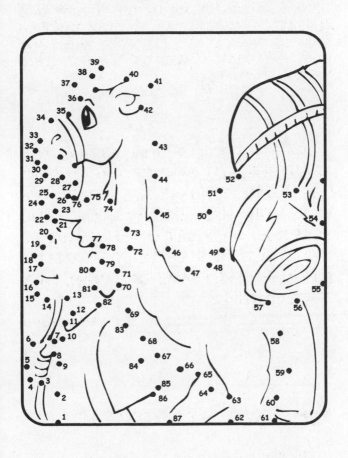

FINISH *the* VERSE

USE THE CODE CHART BELOW TO FINISH THE VERSES ON THE NEXT PAGE. (EXAMPLE: K=24)

	1	2	3	4	5	6	7
1	A	B	C	D	E	F	G
2	H	I	J	K	L	M	N
3	O	P	Q	R	S	T	U
4	V	W	X	Y	Z		

JOKE BREAK:

What do you call Batman after
he's been flattened by a steamroller?
Flatman

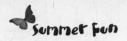

"THEREFORE, SINCE WE HAVE
BEEN __ __ __ __ __ __ __ __ __
     23 37 35 36 22 16 22 15 14

THROUGH __ __ __ __ __ , WE
         16 11 22 36 21

HAVE __ __ __ __ __ WITH GOD
    32 15 11 13 15

THROUGH OUR __ __ __ __ JESUS
         25 31 34 14

CHRIST, THROUGH WHOM WE
HAVE GAINED ACCESS BY FAITH
INTO THIS __ __ __ __ __ IN
        17 34 11 13 15

WHICH WE NOW __ __ __ __ __."
            35 36 11 27 14

ROMANS 5:1–2

CROSSWORD

GALATIANS 3:22–24

ACROSS

1. "BUT THE SCRIPTURE DECLARES THAT THE WHOLE WORLD IS A _____ OF SIN."
2. "SO THAT WHAT WAS _____."
3. "BEING GIVEN THROUGH FAITH IN _____ CHRIST."
4. "MIGHT BE GIVEN TO THOSE _____ BELIEVE."

DOWN

1. " BEFORE THIS FAITH CAME, WE WERE HELD _____ BY THE LAW."
2. "LOCKED UP UNTIL _____ SHOULD BE REVEALED."
3. "SO THE LAW WAS PUT IN _____ TO LEAD US TO CHRIST."
4. "THAT ___ MIGHT BE JUSTIFIED BY FAITH."

TRIVIA TIME:

Jesus once cured a blind man
by spitting on his eyes.
(Mark 8:23)

FILL *in the* BLANKS

USING THE WORDS BELOW, COMPLETE THE VERSE ON THE NEXT PAGE.

BROTHERS   CONFORMED
FIRSTBORN   PREDESTINED
SON   GOD
LIKENESS   FOREKNEW

....

JOKE BREAK:

Oinkment: medicine for a
pig with sore muscles.

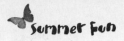

"FOR   THOSE   _____

_____ HE ALSO

_____ TO BE

_____ TO THE

_____ OF HIS _____,

THAT   HE   MIGHT   BE   THE

_____ AMONG   MANY

_____."

ROMANS 8:29

SCRAMBLED VERSES

UNSCRAMBLE THE WORDS BELOW AND COMPLETE THE VERSE ON THE NEXT PAGE.

"EH IDSA OT METH, 'HIST SI HATW I ODLT UYO IHELW I WSA LITSL TWIH UYO: IYVETGNHRE UTMS EB LLUFLDEIF AHTT SI TEWNIRT OATUB EM IN HET LWA FO OESSM, ETH SPRPHTEO DAN HET MASLPS.'"

TRIVIA TIME:

God is a whistler.
(Isaiah 5:26; 7:18)

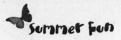

"—— —— —— —— ——,
· —— —— —— —— ——
—— —— —— —— ——
—— —— —— ——
—— —— : —— ——
—— —— —— ——
—— —— —— ——
—— —— —— —— ——
—— —— —— ——,
—— —— —— ——
—— —— ——.'"

LUKE 24:44

WORD LIST

(place)_____

(name of person)_____

(adjective)_____

(verb)_____

(verb)_____

(noun)_____

(number)_____

(verb)_____

(plural noun)_____

(plural noun)_____

(plural noun)_____

(adjective)_____

RIDDLER:

What can run but will not walk,
has a mouth but will not talk,
has a bed but will not sleep?
A river.

MY DREAM VACATION

If I could go anywhere on vacation, I'd

go to _____. I would take
         (PLACE)

_____ and we would fly on a
(NAME OF PERSON)

_____ airplane.
    (ADJECTIVE)

While we were there, we would

_____ different kinds of food
    (VERB)

and _____ many different
         (VERB)

places. We'd also be sure to swim in the

_____.
    (NOUN)

We would spend _____ days
                    (NUMBER)

there, then _____ back home
                 (VERB)

with many _____ and
              (PLURAL NOUN)

_____. There would be many
   (PLURAL NOUN)

stories to tell our _____, and
                        (PLURAL NOUN)

we would remember our trip for a

_____ time.
    (ADJECTIVE)

SCRAMBLED CIRCLES

ON THE NEXT PAGE, UNSCRAMBLE THE WORDS IN THE LIST BELOW. THEN USE THE CIRCLED LETTERS TO COMPLETE THE VERSE.

1. LDSO
2. ERDA
3. IHRTCS
4. WLA
5. VATNOENC
6. LARYRE
7. GEELA
8. EDDI

 TWIST YOUR TONGUE:

Chip chopped chuck for chipped chuck soup.
Chipped chuck soup was chopped by Chip.

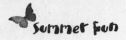

1. _ _ _ ◯

2. _ _ _ ◯

3. ◯ _ _ _ _ _ _

4. ◯ _ _

5. _ _ _ _ _ ◯ _ _

6. _ _ ◯ _ _ _

7. ◯ _ _ _ _

8. _ _ _ ◯

"THEREFORE NO ONE WILL BE
_ _ _ _ _ _ _ _ RIGHTEOUS IN
HIS SIGHT BY OBSERVING THE LAW;
RATHER, THROUGH THE LAW WE BECOME
CONSCIOUS OF SIN."

ROMANS 3:20

I AM A NEW CREATION

USING THE LINES ON THE NEXT PAGE, UNSCRAMBLE THE UNDERLINED WORDS BELOW. THEN FIND THEM IN THE WORD SEARCH PUZZLE.

"<u>ETRHOEFRE</u>, IF <u>NAENOY</u> IS IN CHRIST, HE IS A <u>WEN</u> <u>OCNRIETA</u>; THE <u>DOL</u> HAS GONE, THE NEW HAS <u>EOCM</u>!"

2 CORINTHIANS 5:17

RIDDLER:

What can run on the floor even though it doesn't have legs?
Water

34

Summer fun

_____ _____

_____ _____

_____ _____

```
C O B P Q C E O T A C I
E O C E G R O R B N Q J
R S M A N E H J E Y S D
V P K E B A X D A O T E
O L D L T T T Y B N D E
N R J I S I A D B E L G
T W E R J O V D E N B O
F P J O J N B O N E W S
J Q D H T O B R S J E P
T H E R E F O R E P V E
```

JOB PASSES

"IN ALL THIS, JOB DID NOT SIN BY CHARGING GOD WITH WRONGDOING."

JOB 1:22

AS YOU GO THROUGH THE MAZE ON THE NEXT PAGE, COLLECT THE LETTERS AND UNSCRAMBLE THEM BELOW.

— — —

 TRIVIA TIME:

Abraham had two nephews named
Uz and Buz. (Genesis 22:21)

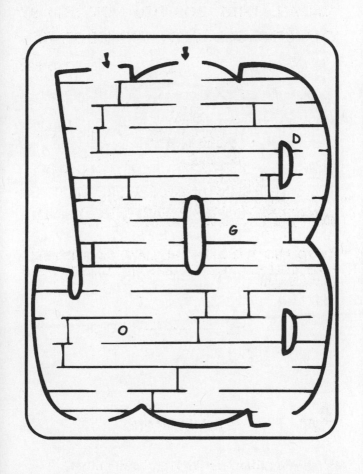

THe LORD APPEARED

HOW DID THE LORD APPEAR TO ABRAM?

"ABRAM TRAVELED THROUGH THE LAND AS FAR AS THE SITE OF THE GREAT TREE OF MOREH AT SHECHEM. AT THAT TIME THE CANAANITES WERE IN THE LAND. THE LORD APPEARED TO ABRAM AND SAID, 'TO YOUR OFFSPRING I WILL GIVE THIS LAND.' SO HE BUILT AN ALTAR THERE TO THE LORD, WHO HAD APPEARED TO HIM."

GENESIS 12:6–7

JOKE BREAK:

What did one clock say to the other?
You tock too much.

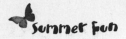

FINISH *the* VERSE

USE THE CODE CHART BELOW TO FINISH THE
VERSE ON THE NEXT PAGE. (EXAMPLE: K=24)

	1	2	3	4	5	6	7
1	A	B	C	D	E	F	G
2	H	I	J	K	L	M	N
3	O	P	Q	R	S	T	U
4	V	W	X	Y	Z		

TRIVIA TIME:

Methuselah lived longer than anyone else whose
age is recorded in the Bible—969 years.
(Genesis 5:27)

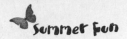
"FOR   YOU   DID   NOT

___ ___ ___ ___ ___ ___ ___   A
34 15 13 15 22 41 15

___ ___ ___ ___ ___ ___   THAT MAKES
35 32 22 34 22 36

YOU A ___ ___ ___ ___ ___ AGAIN TO
        35 25 11 41 15

___ ___ ___ ___, BUT YOU RECEIVED
16 15 11 34

THE ___ ___ ___ ___ ___ ___ OF
      35 32 22 34 22 36

___ ___ ___ ___ ___ ___ ___. AND BY
35 31 27 35 21 22 32

HIM WE ___ ___ ___, '___ ___ ___ ___,
        13 34 44   11 12 12 11

FATHER.'"

ROMANS 8:15

41

CROSSWORD

MATTHEW 5:17-18

ACROSS

1. "'DO NOT _____ THAT I HAVE COME.'"
2. "'TO _____ THE LAW OR THE PROPHETS.'"
3. "'I HAVE NOT COME TO ABOLISH _____.'"
4. "'BUT TO FULFILL _____.'"

DOWN

1. "'I TELL YOU THE TRUTH, UNTIL HEAVEN AND EARTH _____.'"
2. "'NOT THE SMALLEST _____, NOT THE LEAST STROKE OF A PEN.'"
3. "'WILL BY ANY _____ DISAPPEAR FROM THE LAW.'"
4. "'_____ EVERYTHING IS ACCOMPLISHED.'"

 TWIST YOUR TONGUE:

Never freeze three breezy
cheeses when sneezing.

FILL *in the* BLANKS

USING THE WORDS BELOW, COMPLETE THE VERSES ON THE NEXT PAGE.

CREATION
DEATH
SEPARATE
ANGELS
POWERS
CONVINCED

GOD
LIFE
LOVE
PRESENT
HEIGHT
DEMONS

JOKE BREAK:

Where's the best place to park dogs?
In the barking lot

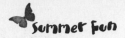

"FOR I AM _____ THAT

NEITHER _____ NOR _____,

NEITHER _____ NOR

_____, NEITHER THE

_____ NOR THE FUTURE, NOR

ANY _____, NEITHER _____

NOR DEPTH, NOR ANYTHING ELSE IN

ALL _____, WILL BE ABLE TO

_____ US FROM THE

_____ OF _____ THAT IS IN

CHRIST JESUS OUR LORD."

ROMANS 8:38–39

SCRAMBLED VERSES

UNSCRAMBLE THE WORDS BELOW AND COMPLETE THE VERSES ON THE NEXT PAGE.

"EW ONWK TATH HET AWL SI TRPAIISUL; TUB I MA PTLUIUAISNR, LODS SA A VSLEA OT ISN. I OD TON NSDNRDUETA AWTH I OD. RFO TAHW I NWTA OT OD I OD OTN OD, UBT WTAH I TEHA I OD. DAN FI I OD ATHW I OD ONT TANW OT OD, I EARGE ATTH ETH LWA SI ODOG. SA TI SI, TI SI ON GLEORN I EYFSML HWO OD TI, TBU TI SI NSI VGIILN NI EM."

TRIVIA TIME:

Once Jesus called demons out of a man and sent them into a herd of about 2,000 pigs. (Mark 5:13)

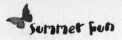

"____ ____ ____ ____
____ ____ ____ ; ____
___ ___ ____ ,
____ ____ ____
____ ___ . ___ ____
____ ____ ____
__ . ____ ___ ____
___ ___ ___ ___
__ . ____ ___ ___ ___
____ ____ ____
___ __ , ___ ____
____ ____ ___ .
___ __ __ , ___ ____ ___
____ ____ ____
__ __ , ___ ___ ___
___ ___ ____ ___ ."

ROMANS 7:14 –17

47

WORD LIST

(verb) _____

(verb) _____

(verb) _____

(verb) _____

(adjective) _____

(noun) _____

(noun) _____

(verb) _____

(noun) _____

(verb) _____

(adjective) _____

(plural noun) _____

(verb) _____

RIDDLER:

What gets larger if you take
anything away from it?
A hole.

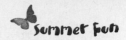

THINGS I DO TO HELP AROUND THE HOUSE

_____ my room and _____
　(VERB)　　　　　　　　　　　　　　(VERB)
my bed.

Help _____ dinner.
　　　　　(VERB)

_____ the _____ dishes
　(VERB)　　　　　　　　(ADJECTIVE)
and put them in the _____.
　　　　　　　　　　　　　(NOUN)

Take out the _____.
　　　　　　　　　　(NOUN)

_____ the car.
　(VERB)

Take the _____ for a walk.
　　　　　　　(NOUN)

_____ the _____
　(VERB)　　　　　　　　(ADJECTIVE)
laundry.

Vacuum the _____.
　　　　　　　　(PLURAL NOUN)

_____ the furniture.
　(VERB)

SCRAMBLED CIRCLES

ON THE NEXT PAGE, UNSCRAMBLE THE WORDS
IN THE LIST BELOW. THEN USE THE CIRCLED
LETTERS TO COMPLETE THE VERSE.

1. EBRO

2. LTUTRYE

3. VCEEEDI

4. DGOO

5. NESMA

6. IFLE

JOKE BREAK:

What do you call a boy cow taking a nap?
A bulldozer

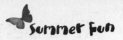

1. _ _ ◯ _

2. _ _ _ ◯ _ _ _

3. _ _ ◯ _ _ _

4. _ ◯ _ _

5. ◯ _ _ _ _

6. _ _ _ ◯

"DID THAT WHICH IS GOOD, THEN,
_ _ _ _ _ _ DEATH TO ME?
BY NO MEANS."

ROMANS 7:13

51

CHRIST LIVES IN ME

FIND THE WORDS UNDERLINED BELOW IN THE WORD SEARCH ON THE NEXT PAGE.

"I HAVE BEEN <u>CRUCIFIED</u> WITH CHRIST AND I NO <u>LONGER</u> LIVE, BUT CHRIST <u>LIVES</u> IN ME. THE <u>LIFE</u> I LIVE IN THE <u>BODY</u>, I LIVE BY <u>FAITH</u> IN THE <u>SON</u> OF <u>GOD</u>, WHO <u>LOVED</u> ME AND GAVE <u>HIMSELF</u> FOR ME."

GALATIANS 2:20

 TRIVIA TIME:

The shortest chapter in the Bible in Psalm 117. It has two verses.

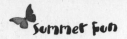
```
H M Q C E V T N S O N L
I R G O Y C D T T U B N
M H I O N T L L W I L O
S D B O D Y K I R E O L
E E K E O L B V E W N G
L P T O L E L E S K G O
F Z L H O M R S T R E D
G A T I V K V S S R R R
S E L T E B I D H I T D
P L I F D N D L I P S A
T W F V B F A I T H K M
R Y E B B P K S E K T B
W A D B A C H E R D Y I
H H N C R U C I F I E D
G O D R S I T I N H I L
```

TEACH ME

"'TEACH ME, AND I WILL BE QUIET;
SHOW ME WHERE I HAVE BEEN WRONG.
HOW PAINFUL ARE HONEST WORDS!
BUT WHAT DO YOUR ARGUMENTS
PROVE?'"

JOB 6:24–25

 TWIST YOUR TONGUE:

The skunk sat on the stump.
The stump said the skunk stunk.
The skunk said the stump stunk.
Who stunk?

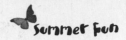
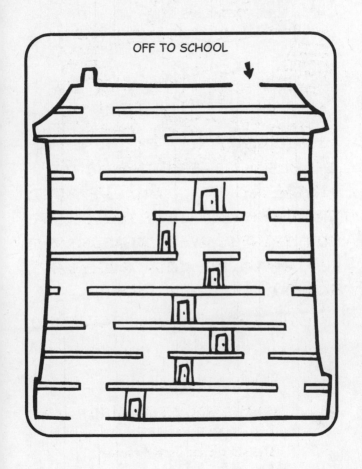

OFF TO SCHOOL

DUST OF THE EARTH

GOD SOMETIMES GIVES WHAT APPEAR TO BE *IMPOSSIBLE* PROMISES. BUT. . .ALL THINGS ARE POSSIBLE WITH GOD.

"'I WILL MAKE YOUR OFFSPRING LIKE THE DUST OF THE EARTH, SO THAT IF ANYONE COULD COUNT THE DUST, THEN YOUR OFFSPRING COULD BE COUNTED. GO, WALK THROUGH THE LENGTH AND BREADTH OF THE LAND, FOR I AM GIVING IT TO YOU.'"

GENESIS 13:16–17

JOKE BREAK:

What kind of lights did Noah put on the ark?
Floodlights

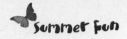

FINISH *the* VERSE

USE THE CODE CHART BELOW TO FINISH THE
VERSE ON THE NEXT PAGE. (EXAMPLE: K=24)

	1	2	3	4	5	6	7
1	A	B	C	D	E	F	G
2	H	I	J	K	L	M	N
3	O	P	Q	R	S	T	U
4	V	W	X	Y	Z		

TRIVIA TIME:

David pretended to be insane once by marking
up a door and drooling all over his beard.
(1 Samuel 21:13)

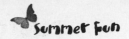

"HE WHO DID $\underline{}_{27}$ $\underline{}_{31}$ $\underline{}_{36}$ HIS OWN

$\underline{}_{35}$ $\underline{}_{32}$ $\underline{}_{11}$ $\underline{}_{34}$ $\underline{}_{15}$ HIS OWN

$\underline{}_{35}$ $\underline{}_{31}$ $\underline{}_{27}$, BUT GAVE $\underline{}_{21}$ $\underline{}_{22}$ $\underline{}_{26}$

UP FOR US $\underline{}_{11}$ $\underline{}_{25}$ $\underline{}_{25}$ —HOW

WILL HE NOT $\underline{}_{11}$ $\underline{}_{25}$ $\underline{}_{35}$ $\underline{}_{31}$,

ALONG WITH $\underline{}_{21}$ $\underline{}_{22}$ $\underline{}_{26}$,

$\underline{}_{17}$ $\underline{}_{34}$ $\underline{}_{11}$ $\underline{}_{13}$ $\underline{}_{22}$ $\underline{}_{31}$ $\underline{}_{37}$ $\underline{}_{35}$ $\underline{}_{25}$ $\underline{}_{44}$

GIVE US ALL $\underline{}_{36}$ $\underline{}_{21}$ $\underline{}_{22}$ $\underline{}_{27}$ $\underline{}_{17}$ $\underline{}_{35}$?"

ROMANS 8:32

CROSSWORD

ACROSS

1. "HE DID NOT ENTER BY _____ OF THE BLOOD OF GOATS AND CALVES."
2. "BUT HE _____ THE MOST HOLY PLACE ONCE FOR ALL."
3. "BY HIS OWN _____."
4. "_____ OBTAINED ETERNAL REDEMPTION."

DOWN

1. "HOW MUCH _____, THEN, WILL THE BLOOD OF CHRIST."
2. "WHO THROUGH THE _____ SPIRIT OFFERED HIMSELF UNBLEMISHED TO GOD."
3. "CLEANSE OUR CONSCIENCES FROM ACTS THAT LEAD TO _____."
4. "SO THAT WE MAY SERVE THE LIVING _____!"

....

JOKE BREAK:

What is a bird's favorite food?
Chocolate chirp cookies

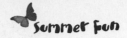

FILL *in the* BLANKS

USING THE WORDS BELOW, COMPLETE THE
VERSES ON THE NEXT PAGE.

TRUSTS
SAVED
NAME
CALLS
BLESSES

SHAME
DIFFERENCE
GENTILE
LORD
SCRIPTURE

TRIVIA TIME:

The iron point on Goliath's spear
weighed about 15 pounds.
(1 Samuel 17:7)

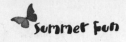

"AS THE _____ SAYS,
'ANYONE WHO _____ IN HIM
WILL NEVER BE PUT TO _____.'
FOR THERE IS NO _____
BETWEEN JEW AND _____—THE
SAME _____ IS LORD OF ALL AND
RICHLY _____ ALL WHO
CALL ON HIM, FOR, 'EVERYONE WHO
_____ ON THE _____ OF THE
LORD WILL BE _____.'"

ROMANS 10:11–13

SCRAMBLED VERSES

UNSCRAMBLE THE WORDS BELOW AND COMPLETE THE VERSES ON THE NEXT PAGE.

"NI IMH EW VEAH TERDPONIME HUHTOGR SHI ODOLB, ETH GESEIOFVSNR FO NSIS, NI NRCOAEADCC TIHW HTE EICSHR FO D'GSO EAGRC TATH EH AHDVSELI NO SU TIHW LAL OSWIDM DNA NDRUTIEAGNSND."

 ## TWIST YOUR TONGUE:

If rustlers wrestle wrestlers
While rustlers rustle rustles,
Could rustlers rustle wrestlers
While wrestlers wrestle rustlers?

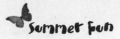

"___ ___ ___ ___

___ ___

___ ___, ___

___ ___,

___ ___

___ ___ ___

___ ___

___ ___ ___

___ ___ ___

___ ___ ___ ___

___ ."

EPHESIANS 1:7-8

WORD LIST

(adjective) _____

(adjective) _____

(plural noun) _____

(number) _____

(adjective) _____

(adjective) _____

(adjective) _____

(noun) _____

(noun) _____

(noun) _____

(number) _____

(plural noun) _____

(number) _____

RIDDLER

Which month of the year
has twenty-eight days?
All of them.

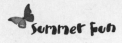
CLASSIC STORIES

_____ _____ Riding
(ADJECTIVE)   (ADJECTIVE)
Hood

The Three Little _____
(PLURAL NOUN)

Goldilocks and the _____ Bears
(NUMBER)

_____ Beauty
(ADJECTIVE)

The _____ Mouse and the
(ADJECTIVE)

_____ Mouse
(ADJECTIVE)

Jack and the _____
(NOUN)

The Gingerbread _____
(NOUN)

The Princess and the _____
(NOUN)

Snow White and the _____
(NUMBER)

_____
(PLURAL NOUN)

The _____ Musketeers
(NUMBER)

67

SCRAMBLED CIRCLES

ON THE NEXT PAGE, UNSCRAMBLE THE WORDS IN THE LIST BELOW. THEN USE THE CIRCLED LETTERS TO COMPLETE THE VERSE.

1. ETJUIDISF

2. WLA

3. LILW

4. CIRTSH

5. UHTOHGR

JOKE BREAK:

Why should you never tell a secret in a cornfield?
Because the stalks have ears

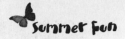
1. _ _ _ _ _ ◯ _ _ _

2. _ ◯ _

3. _ ◯ _ _

4. _ _ _ _ _ ◯

5. _ ◯ _ _ _ _

"KNOW THAT A MAN IS NOT JUSTIFIED
BY OBSERVING THE LAW, BUT BY
__ __ __ __ __ IN JESUS CHRIST."

GALATIANS 2:16

KEEP MY EYES ON JESUS

USING THE LINES ON THE NEXT PAGE, UNSCRAMBLE THE UNDERLINED WORDS BELOW. THEN FIND THEM IN THE WORD SEARCH PUZZLE.

"LET US FIX OUR <u>SEEY</u> ON JESUS, THE <u>RUOAHT</u> AND <u>EPRETFRCE</u> OF OUR <u>TFHAI</u>, WHO FOR THE JOY SET BEFORE HIM <u>REDNEDU</u> THE CROSS, SCORNING ITS SHAME, AND SAT DOWN AT THE RIGHT HAND OF THE <u>NTEHOR</u> OF GOD."

HEBREWS 12:2

....

TRIVIA TIME:

It didn't rain in the Garden of Eden. Water came up from the ground to make things grow.
(Genesis 2:5–6)

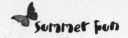

_____ _____

_____ _____

_____ _____

```
S O B P Q F E R E A C I
E Y E S G A O J A F Q J
R S T A N I H D B J S D
V P K A B T H R O N E A
A B Y L T H T D E M D U
P E R F E C T E R B L T
T W E R J U V O S N B H
F P J O J G B R V S F O
J E N D U R E D C J E R
T M E C C P L B T P V E
```

SHOUTS OF JOY

"'SURELY GOD DOES NOT REJECT A BLAMELESS MAN OR STRENGTHEN THE HANDS OF EVILDOERS. HE WILL YET FILL YOUR MOUTH WITH LAUGHTER AND YOUR LIPS WITH SHOUTS OF JOY.'"

JOB 8:20–21

AS YOU GO THROUGH THE MAZE ON THE NEXT PAGE, COLLECT THE LETTERS AND UNSCRAMBLE THEM BELOW.

— — — — —

 JOKE BREAK:

What do you call a flying monkey?
A hot-air baboon

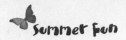

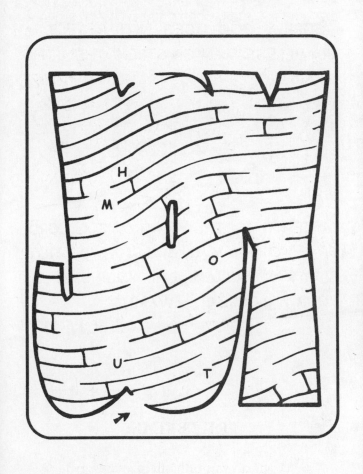

DO NOT BE AFRAID

HAVE YOU EVER WONDERED WHAT A *VISION* IS? IS IT A DREAM OR IS IT LIKE WATCHING A MOVIE?

"AFTER THIS, THE WORD OF THE LORD CAME TO ABRAM IN A VISION: 'DO NOT BE AFRAID, ABRAM. I AM YOUR SHIELD, YOUR VERY GREAT REWARD.'"

GENESIS 15:1

TRIVIA TIME:

Joash was only seven years old when he became king.
(2 Chronicles 24:1)

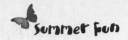

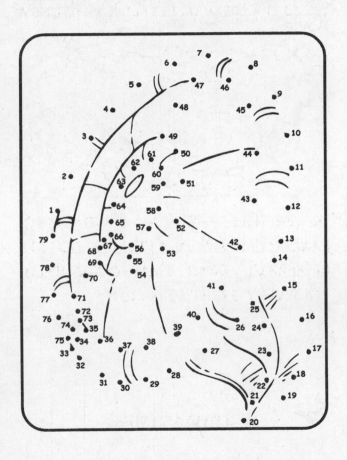

FINISH *the* VERSE

USE THE CODE CHART BELOW TO FINISH THE
VERSE ON THE NEXT PAGE. (EXAMPLE: K=24)

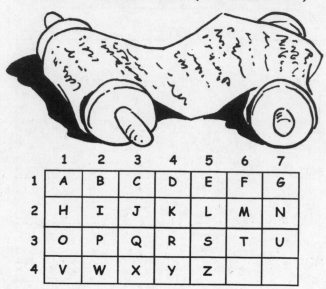

	1	2	3	4	5	6	7
1	A	B	C	D	E	F	G
2	H	I	J	K	L	M	N
3	O	P	Q	R	S	T	U
4	V	W	X	Y	Z		

 TWIST YOUR TONGUE:

Sneaky thieves seized the skis.

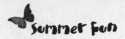

" _ _ _ DID NOT _ _ _ _ _ _
  17 31 14   34 15 23 15 13 36

HIS _ _ _ _ _ _, WHOM HE
    32 15 31 32 25 15

_ _ _ _ _ _ _ _ _. DON'T YOU KNOW
16 31 34 15 24 27 15 42

WHAT THE _ _ _ _ _ _ _ _ _
             35 13 34 22 32 36 37 34 15

SAYS IN THE _ _ _ _ _ _ _ _
               32 11 35 35 11 17 15

ABOUT _ _ _ _ _ _ — HOW HE
       15 25 22 23 11 21

_ _ _ _ _ _ _ _ TO _ _ _
11 32 32 15 11 25 15 14   17 31 14

AGAINST ISRAEL."

ROMANS 11:2

77

CROSSWORD

COLOSSIANS 2:20–22

ACROSS

1. "SINCE YOU DIED WITH CHRIST TO THE BASIC _____ OF THIS WORLD."
2. "WHY, AS THOUGH YOU STILL _____ TO IT."
3. "DO YOU SUBMIT TO ITS _____."
4. "'DO NOT HANDLE! DO NOT TASTE! DO NOT _____!'?"

DOWN

1. "THESE ARE ALL _____."
2. "TO _____ WITH USE."
3. "BECAUSE THEY _____ BASED."
4. "ON HUMAN COMMANDS AND _____."

RIDDLER:

What can travel around the world while
spending its life in a corner?
A postage stamp

FILL *in the* BLANKS

USING THE WORDS BELOW, COMPLETE THE VERSE ON THE NEXT PAGE.

PLEASE	STRONG
BUILD	BEAR
SHOULD	FAILINGS
GOOD	WEAK
NEIGHBOR	OURSELVES

TRIVIA TIME:

Moses had a bronze serpent
that could heal snakebites.
(Numbers 21:6–9)

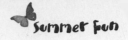

"WE WHO ARE _____ OUGHT

TO _____ WITH THE

_____ OF THE

_____ AND NOT TO PLEASE

_____. EACH OF US

_____ _____ HIS

_____ FOR HIS

_____, TO _____ HIM UP."

ROMANS 15:1–2

SCRAMBLED VERSES

UNSCRAMBLE THE WORDS BELOW AND COMPLETE THE VERSE ON THE NEXT PAGE.

"RFOEEHTER, STJU SA NSI EDTEREN
HET LODWR GTOHUHR EON NMA,
DAN TEHAD RHUTGOH INS, NAD NI
STHI AYW AHDET MEAC OT LAL NME,
SCBEAEU LAL DISNEN—RFO FEORBE
ETH WLA SWA VNGEI, ISN ASW NI
EHT LODWR."

....

 JOKE BREAK:

Cashew: the way nuts sneeze.

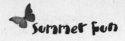

"_____, _____

_____ _____ _____

_____ _____ _____

_____ ____ _____, _____ _____

_____ _____, ____

_____ _____

_____ _____ _____

_____ ____ _____, _____

_____ _____ __

_____ _____ ___

_____ ____ _____ _____

_____ ____ _____, ___

_____ ____ ____ _____ _____

_____."

ROMANS 5:12–13

WORD LIST

(adjective) _____
(adjective) _____
(plural noun) _____
(adjective) _____
(adjective) _____
(verb) _____
(verb) _____
(noun) _____
(noun) _____
(verb) _____
(noun) _____
(noun) _____
(adjective) _____
(adjective) _____
(plural noun) _____
(adjective) _____

RIDDLER:

When does Friday come before Thursday?
In the dictionary.

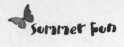

Summer months are _____!
(ADJECTIVE)

There's no school, and it's _____
(ADJECTIVE)
enough outside to wear _____.
(PLURAL NOUN)

On _____ days, it's fun to go
(ADJECTIVE)
to the _____ pool. I love to
(ADJECTIVE)
_____ and _____ off
(VERB)   (VERB)
the diving _____.
(NOUN)

I also like to go to the _____ and
(NOUN)
_____ on the playground, ride
(VERB)
my _____, or throw a
(NOUN)
_____ with my friends.
(NOUN)

When it gets _____ outside, I
(ADJECTIVE)
catch _____ bugs and listen to
(ADJECTIVE)
the _____ chirping.
(PLURAL NOUN)

The summer months are my _____
(ADJECTIVE)
ones!

SCRAMBLED CIRCLES

ON THE NEXT PAGE, UNSCRAMBLE THE WORDS IN THE LIST BELOW. THEN USE THE CIRCLED LETTERS TO COMPLETE THE VERSE.

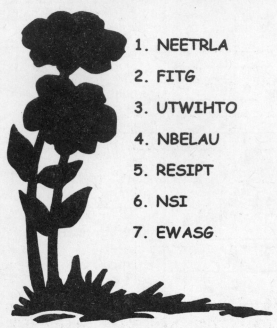

1. NEETRLA

2. FITG

3. UTWIHTO

4. NBELAU

5. RESIPT

6. NSI

7. EWASG

TRIVIA TIME:

The prophet Balaam was once saved from death by a talking donkey. (Numbers 22:21–33)

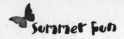

1. _ _ _ _ _ ◯ _

2. _ _ _ ◯

3. _ _ _ _ ◯ _ _

4. _ ◯ _ _ _ _

5. _ _ ◯ _ _ _ _

6. _ _ ◯

7. _ _ ◯ _ _

"HE IS THE _ _ _ _ _ _ _
SACRIFICE FOR OUR SINS, AND NOT
ONLY FOR OURS BUT ALSO FOR THE SINS
OF THE WHOLE WORLD."

1 JOHN 2:2

I AM BEING TRANSFORMED

FIND THE WORDS UNDERLINED BELOW IN THE WORD SEARCH ON THE NEXT PAGE.

"DO NOT <u>CONFORM</u> ANY <u>LONGER</u> TO THE <u>PATTERN</u> OF THIS WORLD, BUT BE <u>TRANSFORMED</u> BY THE <u>RENEWING</u> OF YOUR <u>MIND</u>. THEN YOU WILL BE ABLE TO <u>TEST</u> AND <u>APPROVE</u> WHAT GOD'S WILL IS—HIS GOOD, <u>PLEASING</u> AND <u>PERFECT</u> WILL."

ROMANS 12:2

 TWIST YOUR TONGUE:

Six slippery snails, slid slowly seaward.

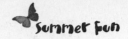
```
T M Q C E V T N W I K M
F R G P E R F E C T I N
T H A O N T L D W N L O
O D B N S E K T D E H L
R E K E S L B G E W O O
E P A O R F L X S K U N
N Z P H V M O F T R L G
E A P I B K V R S R D E
W E R T I B M D M I T R
I L O F A R D L I E S A
N W V V O T E M S T D M
G Y E F B P K S T K T B
W A N B A C H E R E Y I
H O P L E A S I N G S T
C A P A T T E R N H I T
```

PG. 5

"I AM NOT A S H A M E D
OF THE G O S P E L,
BECAUSE IT IS THE
P O W E R OF G O D FOR
THE S A L V A T I O N
OF E V E R Y O N E WHO
BELIEVES: FIRST FOR THE J E W,
THEN FOR THE G E N T I L E."

ROMANS 1:16

PG. 7

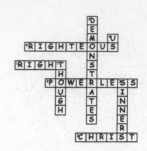

PG. 9

"FOR IN THIS HOPE WE WERE
SAVED. BUT HOPE THAT IS
SEEN IS NO HOPE AT ALL.
WHO HOPES FOR WHAT HE
ALREADY HAS? BUT IF WE HOPE FOR
WHAT WE DO NOT YET
HAVE, WE WAIT FOR IT
PATIENTLY."

ROMANS 8:24-25

PG. 11

" IS THE LAW
THEREFORE OPPOSED
TO THE PROMISES
OF GOD? ABSOLUTELY
NOT! FOR IF A LAW
HAD BEEN GIVEN
THAT COULD IMPART
LIFE, THEN RIGHTEOUSNESS
WOULD CERTAINLY HAVE
COME BY THE LAW."

GALATIANS 3:21

PG. 15

1. C A M E
2. M O S E S
3. G I V E N
4. T R Y
5. C H R I S T
6. N E C K S
7. Y O U
8. J E S U S

"SO THEN, JUST AS YOU RECEIVED
CHRIST AS LORD, C O N T I N U E
TO LIVE IN HIM."

COLOSSIANS 2:6

PG. 17

```
M L Y E C D A M J O Y M
N O F L P R P B C K S D
B V M J E J A A Q I E S
G E H S A P T R U N U B
O D A R C V I B R D W S
O M I N E S E T I N S T
D E T M J V N M U E H N
N U R N O O C T B S G Q
E G E N T L E H U S U U
S E U A G N B N M E L F
S R D M M E I W E Y B R
F A I T H F U L C A X U
R N E L P P I C M S I I
H A P P Y V B N D X U T
Y M N Y I S P I R I T R
```

PG. 19

PRAISE THE LORD

<u>W O R S H I P</u>

PG. 23

"THEREFORE, SINCE WE HAVE
BEEN <u>J U S T I F I E D</u>
13 27 26 24 16 22 15 14
THROUGH <u>F A I T H</u>, WE
16 11 22 16 21
HAVE <u>P E A C E</u> WITH GOD
12 15 11 13 15
THROUGH OUR <u>L O R D</u> JESUS
25 31 24 12
CHRIST, THROUGH WHOM WE
HAVE GAINED ACCESS BY FAITH
INTO THIS <u>G R A C E</u> IN
17 24 11 13 15
WHICH WE NOW <u>S T A N D</u>."
35 16 11 17 14

ROMANS 5:1-2

PG. 25

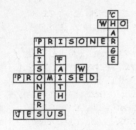

PG. 27

"FOR   THOSE   <u>GOD</u>
<u>FOREKNEW</u> HE ALSO
<u>PREDESTINED</u> TO BE
<u>CONFORMED</u> TO THE
<u>LIKENESS</u> OF HIS <u>SON</u>,
THAT HE MIGHT BE THE
<u>FIRSTBORN</u> AMONG MANY
<u>BROTHERS</u>."

ROMANS 8:29

PG. 29

"<u>HE</u> <u>SAID</u> <u>TO</u> <u>THEM</u>,
<u>THIS</u> <u>IS</u> <u>WHAT</u> <u>I</u>
<u>TOLD</u> <u>YOU</u> <u>WHILE</u> <u>I</u>
<u>WAS</u> <u>STILL</u> <u>WITH</u>
<u>YOU</u>: <u>EVERYTHING</u>
<u>MUST</u> <u>BE</u> <u>FULFILLED</u>
<u>THAT</u> <u>IS</u> <u>WRITTEN</u>
<u>ABOUT</u> <u>ME</u> <u>IN</u> <u>THE</u>
<u>LAW</u> <u>OF</u> <u>MOSES</u>
<u>THE</u> <u>PROPHETS</u> <u>AND</u>
<u>THE</u> <u>PSALMS</u>.'"

LUKE 24:44

PG. 33

1. <u>S O L D</u>
2. <u>D A R E</u>
3. <u>C H R I S T</u>
4. <u>L A W</u>
5. <u>C O V E N A N T</u>
6. <u>R A R E L Y</u>
7. <u>E A G L E</u>
8. <u>D I E D</u>

"THEREFORE NO ONE WILL BE
<u>D E C L A R E D</u> RIGHTEOUS IN
HIS SIGHT BY OBSERVING THE LAW;
RATHER, THROUGH THE LAW WE BECOME
CONSCIOUS OF SIN."

ROMANS 3:20

PG. 35

THEREFORE	ANYONE
NEW	CREATION
OLD	COME

```
C O B P Q C E O T A C I
E O C E G R O R B N Q J
R S M A N E H J E Y S D
V P R E B A X D A O T E
O L D L T T T Y B N D E
N R J I S I A D B E L G
T W E R J O V D E N B O
F P J O J N B O N E W S
J Q D H T O B R S J E P
T H E R E F O R E P V E
```

PG. 37

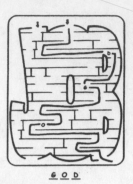

G O D

PG. 41

"FOR YOU DID NOT
<u>R E C E I V E</u> A
_{26 15 13 19 18}
<u>S P I R I T</u> THAT MAKES
YOU A <u>S L A V E</u> AGAIN TO
<u>F E A R</u>, BUT YOU RECEIVED
THE <u>S P I R I T</u> OF
<u>S O N S H I P</u>, AND BY
HIM WE <u>C R Y</u>, '<u>A B B A</u>,
FATHER.'"

ROMANS 8:15

PG. 43

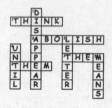

PG. 45

"FOR I AM <u>CONVINCED</u> THAT
NEITHER <u>DEATH</u> NOR <u>LIFE</u>,
NEITHER <u>ANGELS</u> NOR
<u>DEMONS</u>, NEITHER THE
<u>PRESENT</u> NOR THE FUTURE, NOR
ANY <u>POWERS</u>, NEITHER <u>HEIGHT</u>
NOR DEPTH, NOR ANYTHING ELSE IN
ALL <u>CREATION</u>, WILL BE ABLE TO
<u>SEPARATE</u> US FROM THE
<u>LOVE</u> OF <u>GOD</u> THAT IS IN
CHRIST JESUS OUR LORD."

ROMANS 8:38-39

PG. 47

" <u>WE</u> <u>KNOW</u> <u>THAT</u> <u>THE</u>
<u>LAW</u> <u>IS</u> <u>SPIRITUAL</u> ; <u>BUT</u>
<u>I</u> <u>AM</u> <u>UNSPIRITUAL</u> ,
<u>SOLD</u> <u>AS</u> <u>A</u> <u>SLAVE</u>
<u>TO</u> <u>SIN</u>. <u>I</u> <u>DO</u> <u>NOT</u>
<u>UNDERSTAND</u> <u>WHAT</u> <u>I</u>
<u>DO</u>. <u>FOR</u> <u>WHAT</u> <u>I</u> <u>WANT</u>
<u>TO</u> <u>DO</u> <u>I</u> <u>DO</u> <u>NOT</u> <u>DO</u>
<u>BUT</u> <u>WHAT</u> <u>I</u> <u>HATE</u> <u>I</u>
<u>DO</u>. <u>AND</u> <u>IF</u> <u>I</u> <u>DO</u>
<u>WHAT</u> <u>I</u> <u>DO</u> <u>NOT</u> <u>WANT</u>
<u>TO</u> <u>DO</u>, <u>I</u> <u>AGREE</u> <u>THAT</u>
<u>THE</u> <u>LAW</u> <u>IS</u> <u>GOOD</u>.
<u>AS</u> <u>IT</u> <u>IS</u>, <u>IT</u> <u>IS</u> <u>NO</u>
<u>LONGER</u> <u>I</u> <u>MYSELF</u> <u>WHO</u>
<u>DO</u> <u>IT</u>, <u>BUT</u> <u>IT</u> <u>IS</u>
<u>SIN</u> <u>LIVING</u> <u>IN</u> <u>ME</u>."

ROMANS 7:14-17

PG. 51

1. R O B E
2. U T T E R L Y
3. D E C E I V E
4. G O O D
5. M E A N S
6. L I F E

"DID THAT WHICH IS GOOD, THEN,
B E C O M E DEATH TO ME?
BY NO MEANS."

ROMANS 7:13

PG. 53

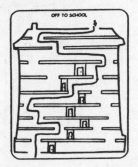

PG. 55

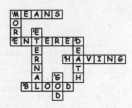

OFF TO SCHOOL

PG. 61

MEANS
MORE
ENTERED
ETERNAL
HAVING
DEATH
GOD
BLOOD

PG. 59

"HE WHO DID N O T
S P A R E HIS OWN
S O N, BUT GAVE H I M
UP FOR US A L L — HOW
WILL HE NOT A L S O,
ALONG WITH H I M,
G R A C I O U S L Y
GIVE US ALL T H I N G S?"

ROMANS 8:32

PG. 63

"AS THE SCRIPTURE SAYS,
'ANYONE WHO TRUSTS IN HIM
WILL NEVER BE PUT TO SHAME.'
FOR THERE IS NO DIFFERENCE
BETWEEN JEW AND GENTILE — THE
SAME LORD IS LORD OF ALL AND
RICHLY BLESSES ALL WHO
CALL ON HIM, FOR, 'EVERYONE WHO
CALLS ON THE NAME OF THE
LORD WILL BE SAVED.'"

ROMANS 10:11-13

PG. 65

" IN HIM WE HAVE
REDEMPTION THROUGH
HIS BLOOD THE
FORGIVENESS OF SINS
IN ACCORDANCE
WITH THE RICHES
OF GOD'S GRACE
THAT HE LAVISHED
ON US WITH
ALL WISDOM AND
UNDERSTANDING "

EPHESIANS 1:7–8

PG. 69

1. J U S T I (F) I E D
2. L (A) W
3. W (I) L L
4. C H R I S (T)
5. I (H) R O U G H

"KNOW THAT A MAN IS NOT JUSTIFIED
BY OBSERVING THE LAW, BUT BY
F A I T H IN JESUS CHRIST."

GALATIANS 2:16

PG. 71

EYES	AUTHOR
PERFECTER	FAITH
ENDURED	THRONE

```
S O B P Q F E R E A C I
E Y E S G A O J A F Q J
R S T A N I H D B J S D
V P K A B T H R O N E A
A B Y L T H T D E M D U
P E R F E C T E R B L T
T W E R J U V O S N B H
F P J O J G B R V S F O
J E N D U R E D C J E R
T M E C C P L B T P V E
```

PG. 73

M O U T H

PG. 77

"G O D DID NOT R E J E C T
HIS P E O P L E, WHOM HE
F O R E K N E W. DON'T YOU KNOW
WHAT THE S C R I P T U R E
SAYS IN THE P A S S A G E
ABOUT E L I J A H – HOW HE
A P P E A L E D TO G O D
AGAINST ISRAEL."

ROMANS 11:2

PG. 79

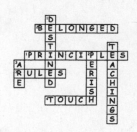

PG. 81

"WE WHO ARE __STRONG__ OUGHT

TO __BEAR__ WITH THE

__FAILINGS__ OF THE

__WEAK__ AND NOT TO PLEASE

__OURSELVES__. EACH OF US

__SHOULD__ __PLEASE__ HIS

__NEIGHBOR__ FOR HIS

__GOOD__ TO __BUILD__ HIM UP."

ROMANS 15:1-2

PG. 83

"__THEREFORE__, __JUST__

__AS__ __SIN__ __ENTERED__

__THE__ __WORLD__ __THROUGH__

__ONE__ __MAN__ __AND__ __DEATH__

__THROUGH__ __SIN__, __AND__

__IN__ __THIS__ __WAY__

__DEATH__ __CAME__ __TO__

__ALL__ __MEN__, __BECAUSE__

__ALL__ __SINNED__ – __FOR__

__BEFORE__ __THE__ __LAW__

__WAS__ __GIVEN__, __SIN__

__WAS__ __IN__ __THE__

ROMANS 5:12-13

PG. 87

1. __E T E R N (A) L__
2. __G I F (T)__
3. __W I T H (O) U T__
4. __U (N) A B L E__
5. __P R (I) E S T__
6. __S I (N)__
7. __W A (G) E S__

"HE IS THE __A T O N I N G__
SACRIFICE FOR OUR SINS, AND NOT
ONLY FOR OURS BUT ALSO FOR THE SINS
OF THE WHOLE WORLD."

1 JOHN 2:2

PG. 89

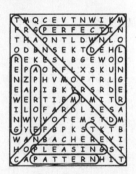